Please check all items for damages
before leaving the Library.
Thereafter you will be held
responsible for all injuries
to items beyond reasonable wear.

Helen M. Plum Memorial Library

Lombard, Illinois

A daily fine will be charged for
overdue materials.

CAPE HATTERAS LIGHT

The Tallest Lighthouse in the United States

AILEEN WEINTRAUB

The Rosen Publishing Group's
PowerKids Press™
New York

To Amy and Ilana, both shining lights

Published in 2003 by The Rosen Publishing Group, Inc.
29 East 21st Street, New York, NY 10010

First Edition

Editors: Leslie Kaplan and Jennifer Landau
Book Design: Maria E. Melendez

Photo credits: Cover and title page photo, p. 4 photo and drawing, p. 5 upper right, p. 6 upper left, p. 7 photo, p. 8 drawing, p. 10 upper left, p. 11 diagrams, p. 12, p. 13 upper right, p. 15, p. 16, p. 18 upper left, p. 19, p. 20, p. 21 upper right, p. 22 lower right © United States Lighthouse Society; p. 7 (map) © NOAA (National Oceanic and Atmospheric Administration); p. 8, p. 11 (portrait of Augustin Fresnel) © Bettmann/Corbis; cover, title page, backgrounds, and border illustrations by Maria Melendez.

Weintraub, Aileen, 1973–
    Cape Hatteras light: the tallest lighthouse in the United States / Aileen Weintraub.
        p. cm. — (Great lighthouses of North America)
    Includes bibliographical references and index.
    Summary: This is a history of North Carolina's Cape Hatteras Lighthouse, the tallest lighthouse in the United States and the second tallest lighthouse in the world.
        ISBN 0-8239-6168-0 (lib.)
        1. Cape Hatteras Lighthouse (N.C.)—Juvenile literature [1. Cape Hatteras Lighthouse (N.C.)   2. Lighthouses]   I. Title
II. Series
        VK1025.C27 W45 2002   2001-003898
        387.1'55'09756175—dc21

Contents

Left: *Cape Hatteras Light is a famous symbol of North Carolina.*
Right: *This sketch shows the kind of design used for the Hatteras lighthouse.*

The Grand Lady of Lighthouses

Cape Hatteras Light is a lighthouse located on a quiet beach on the Outer Banks of North Carolina. Lighthouses are towers with bright lights on top. They are built along coastlines all around the world to help guide ships. The lighthouse that stands at Cape Hatteras today was completed in 1870. It is the tallest one in the United States and the second-tallest brick lighthouse in the world. From the bottom of its **foundation** to the top of its roof, it measures about 200 feet (61 m). It is known as the Grand Lady of Lighthouses because of its height. This narrow building has 268 steps and more than one million bricks.

This is the Hatteras beacon, a light signal that stood separately from the lighthouse. It was probably used to guide ships that were already safely inside the Hatteras cove.

5

The Graveyard of the Atlantic

The Outer Banks is known for its stormy weather. Probably more than 1,000 ships have crashed there. Accidents happen because the passage around Cape Hatteras is narrow and hard to see. Sand shifts under the water for more than 10 miles (16 km) from the coast. The changing sandpiles endanger ships. This area is called the Diamond **Shoals**. There are also two strong ocean **currents** that meet at the cape. Ships used the currents to travel faster. To use the currents, ships had to get close to the Outer Banks and the Diamond Shoals. So many ships were wrecked there that the cape was nicknamed the Graveyard of the Atlantic.

Inset: *This is a map of the Diamond Shoals and Cape Hatteras. Many shipwrecks occurred in the rough waters near Cape Hatteras.*

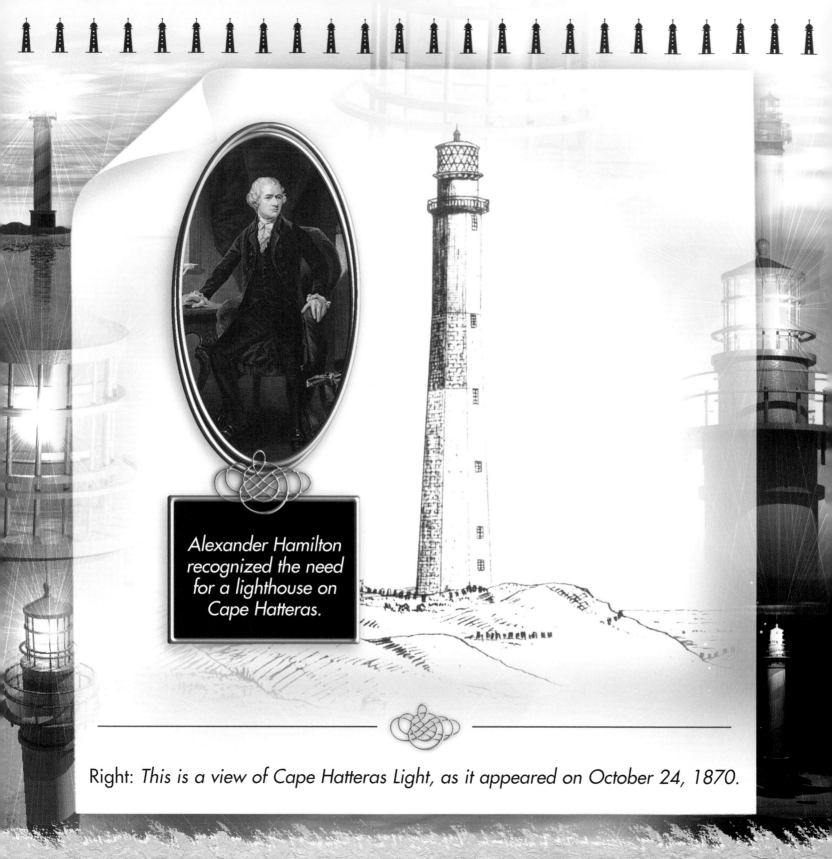

Alexander Hamilton recognized the need for a lighthouse on Cape Hatteras.

Right: *This is a view of Cape Hatteras Light, as it appeared on October 24, 1870.*

A Light Is Born

In 1773, Alexander Hamilton, who would later become one of the leaders of the **American Revolution**, was on a **journey** that took him past Cape Hatteras. During a storm, his ship caught fire, and for 12 hours the crew fought for their lives. Hamilton swore that one day he would build a lighthouse on the cape to guide other ships. In 1794, **Congress** finally approved a permanent lighthouse for the cape. It took almost 10 years to build. This lighthouse was made of **sandstone** and was only 90 feet (27 m) high. The light was lit using whale oil, which did not make the light shine very brightly. Storms could put out the light for days at a time. The Lighthouse Board was created in 1852 to improve all U.S. lighthouses. The board decided to raise the Cape Hatteras tower to 150 feet (46 m) high so it would be easier to see.

A New Type of Light

The Lighthouse Board ordered a lens called a first order Fresnel lens for Cape Hatteras Light. This lens made the light easier to see from greater distances. Augustin Fresnel, a Frenchman, invented the lens in 1822. The Fresnel lens looks like a glass beehive. The glass in the center magnifies the light. The glass above and below the center bends the light. This combination sends out a powerful beam.

The type of light used at Cape Hatteras has changed many times. It was later decided that a turning light would be better than a steady beam. A weight falling from the top of the tower turned the light's gears, which turned the lens.

This is how the Fresnel lens of Cape Hatteras Light appears at night.

10

These diagrams show a Fresnel lens from various angles. Augustin Fresnel (top center) invented this lens, which comes in six different sizes, called orders.

During the Civil War, the Union fleet crossed the stormy waters of the Hatteras Bar, as shown above.

War Closes the Tower

During the **Civil War**, the **Confederate** army wanted to destroy Cape Hatteras Light so the northern states couldn't use it to guide their ships. In 1861, the **Union** army saved the tower from being destroyed. However, Confederate forces took the Fresnel lens. The light couldn't shine without the lens. In 1862, the lighthouse shone again, but it was badly **damaged**. In 1867, Congress set aside $75,000 to build a new lighthouse. This one was built 600 feet (183 m) north of the original. The old lighthouse was torn down. Congress wanted the new one painted with black and white stripes so ships would know their location when passing by during the day.

The Union used Cape Hatteras as a fort during the Civil War. Union troops are shown standing at the base of the lighthouse.

13

The Wind and the Waves

The new tower for Cape Hatteras Light was finally finished in 1870. It cost more than $150,000. A new Fresnel lens was **installed**, and on December 16, 1870, the light was turned on. This brick lighthouse stood 1,500 feet (457 m) from the sea. **Erosion** had always been a big problem at Cape Hatteras. By 1935, waves were washing around the tower. The ocean and the strong winds had washed away all the land. The brick lighthouse was **abandoned** and was replaced with a steel tower 1 mile (1.6 km) **inland**. In the late 1930s, the erosion seemed to stop. On January 23, 1950, the light in the brick tower was turned back on. The National Park Service took over ownership of the brick tower when it was abandoned in 1935. Today the National Park Service keeps up the tower as a historic structure.

Erosion of the land around the lighthouse made it necessary to move the structure away from the coast.

Cape Hatteras Light is the tallest lighthouse in the United States and the second-tallest brick lighthouse in the world.

A Brighter Light

In 1935, the tower shut down for a while because of erosion. When the lighthouse opened again in 1950, the **power source** for its light was changed from oil to electricity. Electricity allowed the light to turn without using a falling weight to move the gears. The electric light that shines today was put in the tower in 1972. It has two 1,000-**watt** lamps. Each lamp has a beam of 800,000 **candlepower**. One candlepower is the amount of light coming from a single candle. That means that each beam of light from Cape Hatteras Light has the brightness of 800,000 candles. The light flashes every 7½ seconds and can be seen for 20 miles (32 km).

Keepers of Hatteras

Lighthouse keepers used to tend the lighthouse and to keep the light burning. They had to wind the gears and trim the light's **wick**. Their job was important. If the light died, that could mean trouble for ships. More than 80 lighthouse keepers have worked at Cape Hatteras. Thomas Jefferson appointed the first keeper at Cape Hatteras in 1802, before the lighthouse was even finished. At Cape Hatteras, the lighthouse keeper had two assistants. The keepers and their families lived in a place called the Keepers' Quarters. The last keeper, Unaka Jennette, ended his term when the light was moved to the steel tower. Advancements in **technology** have made it possible to run lighthouses without keepers.

Keeper Unaka Jennette used to polish the Fresnel lens in the tower at Cape Hatteras. This photo is from the December 1933 issue of National Geographic.

18

This photo of the head keeper's home was taken around 1894.
Today the building houses the Cape Hatteras Light gift shop.

Cape Hatteras Lighthouse

The lighthouse, seen from the beach

The tower on its new foundation

The Keepers' Quarters, relocated

A close-up of the tower on its new foundation

The tower, jacked up and ready to move

Under the lighthouse

The Move of the Century

Once again in the late twentieth century, erosion threatened Cape Hatteras Light. In 1989, the National Academy of Sciences recommended moving the entire lighthouse away from the shore. This move didn't happen until the summer of 1999. The move took 23 days, because the lighthouse weighs 4,400 tons (3,991 t). Engineers, construction workers, and volunteers all helped. They built a platform of steel beams, oak timbers, and rollers. Thousands of people came to watch the move. On the first day, the lighthouse was moved only 10 feet (3 m). Its final location is 2,900 feet (884 m) from its original 1870 location.

The keeper's house was prepared for the move to a location farther inland.

Ghosts and the Sea

Cape Hatteras is a mysterious place. There are legends of ghost ships that appear out of nowhere and float along the sea near the lighthouse. People talk of one ship that was found to have no crew on board, only a gray cat. The beds on the ship were made and food was prepared. No one ever found out what had happened to the sailors or from where the ship came. It became known as the ghost ship of the Diamond Shoals. Another legend tells of a white dolphin named Hatteras Jack that used to rise to the surface of the sea in stormy weather and guide ships to safety. Legends and all, the tallest lighthouse in the United States stands as a reminder of history and hope. Even today it shines brightly in the dark of night.

After being moved, Cape Hatteras Light reopened at its new location in May 2000.

Glossary

abandoned (uh-BAN-dund) Left behind, no longer used.

American Revolution (uh-MER-uh-ken reh-vuh-LOO-shun) A war for freedom that soldiers from the American colonies fought against England.

candlepower (KAN-duhl-pow-uhr) The amount of light coming from one candle.

Civil War (SIH-vul WOR) The war fought between the northern and southern states of America from 1861 to 1865.

Confederate (kun-FEH-duh-ret) The southern states during the Civil War.

Congress (KON-gres) The part of the U.S. government that makes laws.

currents (KUR-ents) The flow of water in a certain direction.

damaged (DAM-ijd) To have been badly hurt.

erosion (ih-ROH-zhun) A slow wearing away or washing away of something.

foundation (fown-DAY-shun) The base on which a structure is built.

inland (IN-land) Land away from a coast or a border.

installed (in-STAWLD) To have set up for use.

journey (JER-nee) A long trip.

legends (LEH-jendz) Stories passed down through the years that many people believe.

power source (POW-er SORS) The energy that lets a machine do its work.

sandstone (SAND-stohn) A kind of rock made up of grains of sand held together by a kind of natural cement.

shoals (SHOHLZ) Places in rivers, lakes, or oceans where the water is shallow.

technology (tek-NAH-luh-jee) Industry that deals with electronics and computers.

Union (YOON-yun) The northern states during the Civil War.

watt (WAHT) A unit for measuring electrical power.

wick (WIHK) A cord in an oil lamp or candle that soaks up the fuel and burns when it is lit.

Index

Web Sites

To learn more about Cape Hatteras, check out these Web sites:

www.insiders.com/outerbanks/sb-wonders.htm
www.cr.nps.gov/maritime/nhl/capehatt.htm